Marketing Math Made Really Easy

A simple approach to the math that makes marketing work

John Story, Ph. D.

ISBN: 0692648380
ISBN-13: 978-0692648384

DEDICATION

This book is dedicated to my three favorite math students, Becca, Megan and Erin Story. They have been fun, inquisitive learners for many years.

Other books by Dr. John Story

Business Short Books
Learning Curves, Economies of Scale, and Strategic Marketing
The Power of Segmentation
Price Elasticity of Demand and Marketing

(Coming Spring '16)
Why Millennials . . .
Why Relationships Matter
What Customer Loyalty Really Means
How Your Product Mix Defines Your Strategy

Non-Business Books
Old Guy Surfing

Contents

ACKNOWLEDGMENTS

I would like to acknowledge my wife, Colleen, whose patience and understanding make this possible. I would also like to recognize the great math teachers I had over the years. I hope they know who they are.

Introduction

In my experience as a professor of marketing, students' least favorite aspect of marketing is marketing math. This is really a shame, because marketing math is not that difficult, and mastering the mathematics of marketing is an easy way to create significant personal competitive advantage. Marketing Math Made Really Easy introduces the calculations marketers need to succeed, as well as tips and tricks for learning them. Whether you are great at math, or avoid it all costs, Marketing Math will make the mathematics of marketing easier for you.

Breakeven Analysis

Breakeven analysis is where all marketing math begins. As with most marketing terms, breakeven is exactly what it says. It is the point at which total income equals total costs. There are no profits, or losses. The firm is breaking even. Students sometimes complain about having to calculate breakeven, because they only want to make profits. "No one," they tell me, "is in business to breakeven." While they are right about that, they are wrong about the value of breakeven analysis. It tells you everything you need to know about being profitable.

At your breakeven point, you are selling just enough, at just the right price, to exactly cover all of your costs. There are two types of cost you need to think about, fixed and variable. Every company has some fixed costs, recurring expenses that don't change based on how much you produce, or sell. Examples are rent, note payments, and cost of administrative personnel. Whether you sell a lot, or a little each month, these expenses are there and stay the same. There are also variable costs, costs that increase and decrease with levels of production. The labor used to produce your product or service is an example of this. Amazon, UPS, and FedEx all have to hire extra employees during the holiday season, to cope with increased demand for their services. Raw materials, parts, and components are another example. If Dell sells more computers, they spend more on processors and keyboards.

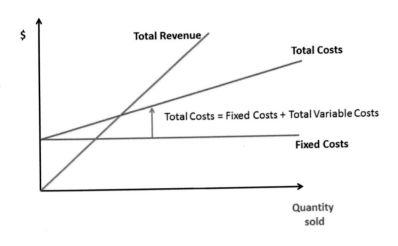

The third component of breakeven analysis is revenue, the income you create by selling your product.

Breakeven begins with selling one unit of your product, at a price above the variable costs required to produce it. This difference between selling price (P) and variable cost (VC) is that unit's contribution.

Contribution = P − VC
P − Selling Price
VC − Variable Costs per Unit

If you sell a product for $15 that costs you $10 to produce, that product contributes $5. That contribution is what you use to cover fixed costs, and then ultimately to create profit. Breakeven is the point at which you have just covered fixed costs.

Profit = Total Revenue - Total Costs
at Break-even, Profit = 0, so
0 = Total Revenue − Total Cost
Total Revenue = Total Cost

(P x Q) = FC + (VC x Q)	Primary Breakeven Equation

P − Selling Price
Q − Quantity sold

FC – Fixed Costs

VC – Variable Costs per Unit

To break that down:

- If you multiply the selling price times the quantity sold (P x Q), you get total revenue.
- If you multiply variable costs per unit times the quantity sold (VC x Q), you get total variable costs.
- When you add fixed costs to total variable costs, you get total cost for that production quantity.
- At the breakeven point, total revenue and total cost are equal.

Example:

Consider a company producing cardboard boxes.

FC = $200,000 per year

VC = $ .50 per box

P = $2.50 per box

How many do they need to sell to break even?

(P x Q) = FC + (VC x Q)

($2.50)Q = $200,000 + ($.50)Q

($2.50)Q - ($.50)Q = $200,000

($2.50 - $.50)Q = $200,000

$$Q = \frac{\$200,000}{\$2} = 100,000$$

They need to sell 100,000 boxes per year to break even.

We can check that result by plugging it back into the formula.

(P x Q) = FC + (VC x Q)

($2.50)(100,000) = $200,000 + ($.50)(100,000)

$250,000 = $250,000

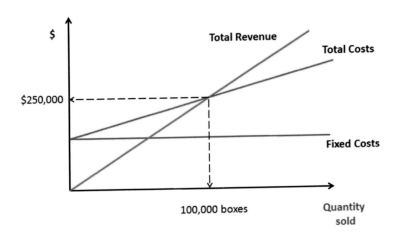

Notice that when solving that problem what we ended up with was the fixed costs divided by the per unit contribution.

$$Q = \frac{\$200,000}{(\$2.50 - \$.50)}$$

If you know fixed costs, variable costs, and selling price, you can simplify the breakeven equation to:

$$Q = \frac{FC}{(P - VC)}$$

Another way this problem might be posed is, if the quantity were known, what selling price would achieve breakeven?

FC = $200,000 per year

VC = $ .50

Q = 300,000

P = ?

(P x Q) = FC + (VC x Q)

P(300,000) = $200,000 + ($.50)300,000

$$P = \frac{\$350,000}{300,000} = \$1.17$$

They would need to sell for about $1.17 each.

We can check that by plugging the numbers back into the equation.

$1.17(300,000) = \$200,000 + \$.50(300,000)$
$\$351,000 \approx \$350,000$

So $1.17 is as close as we can get, we're off $1,000 due to rounding selling price to the nearest penny.

The equation **always** works, but it may help to also think about this problem from a different perspective. Another way to approach this question is to ask how much each box needs to contribute to fixed costs.

$$\frac{200,000}{300,000} = .6667 \; per \; box$$

Since they cost you $.50 to make, you need to sell them for $.50 + $.6667 = $1.17

Contribution per box needs to be $.67 = (P − VC) = (P - $.50), so P = $.6667 + $.50 = $1.17

Breakeven analysis is simply a matter of plugging the right numbers into the equation and performing a little math. It's always important to check your result by plugging everything back into the equation and making sure that total revenue really does equal total costs.

What if instead of just finding the breakeven point, you wanted to calculate the required price, or quantity, at a given profit level? There is a simple trick to this. Simply treat your desired profit as though it were a fixed cost. Consider the example of the box company, given previously.

Example:

Consider a company producing cardboard boxes.

> FC = $200,000 per year
> VC = $ .50
> P = $2.50
> But now, Desired profit = $100,000

How many do they need to achieve that profit level?

(P x Q) = FC + (VC x Q)
($2.50)Q = $200,000 + $100,000 + ($.50)Q
($2.50)Q - ($.50)Q = $300,000
($2.50 - $.50)Q = $300,000

$$Q = \frac{\$300,000}{\$2} = 150,000$$

They need to sell 150,000 boxes per year to make $100,000 in profits. We can check this:

Profit = TR − TC

Profit = 2.5(150,000) − 200,000 - .5(150,000) =
375,000 − 200,000 − 75,000 = $100,000

Notice that they needed to sell 50,000 more boxes, to have $100,000 in profit. Since each box contributes $2, this makes perfect sense.

50,000 x ($2.50 - $2) = $100,000

Breakeven analysis is a very powerful tool, but not perfect. One shortcoming of breakeven analysis is that it only tells you how many you need to sell at a certain price, not whether you actually can. The demand curve and the price elasticity of demand help you answer that question.

Price Elasticity of Demand

Price elasticity of demand is exactly what the name says. It is the elasticity of demand to changes in price. It measures the extent to which the quantity demanded increases, or decreases, when price changes. If demand is elastic and you change price, it stretches, just as a rubber band does when you pull on it.

The formula for price elasticity of demand is simply the ratio of the percentage change in demand to the percentage change in price. Except for a very few odd exceptions, when prices go up, demand goes down, and vice versa. Since prices and demand move in opposite directions, elasticity would always be negative, so we simply use the absolute value.

$$E = \left|\frac{\%\Delta D}{\%\Delta P}\right|$$

E – Elasticity
$\%\Delta D$ – percentage change in Demand
$\%\Delta P$ – percentage change in Price

For instance, if the price of oranges goes down 30% and the quantity demanded increases 20%, the elasticity of demand would be:

$$E = \left|\frac{20\%}{-30\%}\right| = .667$$

Elasticity ranges from zero, when demand does not change when prices change, to infinity, when even a miniscule change in price results in a large change in demand.

One other notable value is when the percentage change in demand is the same as the percentage change in price. Raise price 10% and demand drops 10%. Drop price 20% and demand drops 20%. In that case, elasticity is equal to one, called unitary elastic.

If elasticity is less than one, we say demand is inelastic. If elasticity equals one, we say demand is unitary elastic. If elasticity is greater than one, we say demand is elastic.

Price Elasticity of Demand

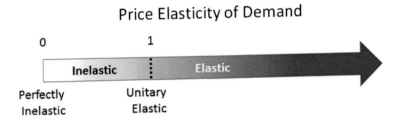

Different Demand Elasticities

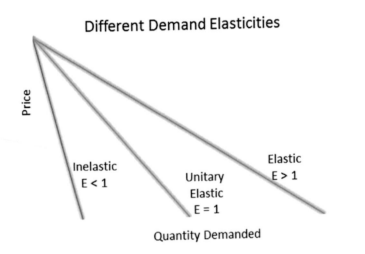

Quantity Demanded

If gasoline increases in price by 20% and demand drops by 5%, since the percentage change in demand is less than the percentage change in price, we know that demand is inelastic.

$$E = \left| \frac{-5\%}{20\%} \right| = .25$$

If the price of chocolate increases by 20% and demand declines 35%, since the percentage change in demand is greater than the percentage change in price, we know demand is elastic.

$$E = \left| \frac{-35\%}{20\%} \right| = 1.75$$

The only question remaining is how to calculate the percentage changes in price and demand.

The most commonly used method to calculate the percentage changes in price and demand is to subtract the new value from the old value and divide that difference by the old value.

$$\%\Delta D = \frac{(D_2 - D_1)}{D_1} \qquad \%\Delta P = \frac{(P_2 - P_1)}{P_1}$$

For example, if the price of oranges went from $1.10 per pound to $1.65 per pound, the percentage change would be:

$$\frac{(1.65 - 1.10)}{1.10} = .5 \; or \; 50\%$$

If demand went from 400 per day to 300 per day, the percentage change would be:

$$\frac{(300 - 400)}{400} = -.25 \; or \; -25\%$$

That would give us a price elasticity of demand of:

$$E = \left| \frac{-25\%}{50\%} \right| = .5$$

Since the elasticity is less than one, demand is inelastic.

This method, called the point elasticity of demand, is sometimes criticized because the same amount of change in the opposite direction gives a different percentage. Going from $1.10 to $1.65 is a 50% increase, but going from $1.65 to $1.10 is only a 33.3% decrease. Going from 400 oranges to 300 is a 25% decrease, while going from 300 to 400 is a 33.3% increase. My personal preference is to use the point elasticity. I believe that it accurately reflects consumers' perceptions. However, you will sometimes see an alternate formula used, the arc elasticity of demand. The only difference is the denominator when calculating the percentage change. Arc elasticity uses the average of the two values. Using the example above:

If the price of oranges went from $1.10 per pound to $1.65 per pound, the percentage change would be:

$$\frac{(1.65 - 1.10)}{((1.10 + 1.65)/2)} = .4 \ or \ 40\%$$

If demand went from 400 per day to 300 per day, the percentage change would be:

$$\frac{(300 - 400)}{((300 - 400)/2)} = -.286 \ or \ -28.6\%$$

That would give us a price elasticity of demand of:

$$E = \left| \frac{-28.6\%}{40\%} \right| = .715$$

Notice that this is a slightly different result from the point elasticity of .5. In both cases demand is inelastic, but is somewhat less inelastic for the arc elasticity calculation.

Arc elasticity of demand will give you more consistent results, particularly when the elasticity is close to 1. It also gives you a nice smooth curve, if you plot the different prices and quantities demanded, while point elasticity does not. However, point elasticity gives you a simple approximation, that may better represent perceptions. My preference is to use the simpler point elasticity, and all of the examples will use that formula. For more on this see my Business Short Book, Price Elasticity of Demand and Marketing.

Example 1:

What if a car dealer, Absolute Autos, reduced prices on all of their cars from an average of $10,000 to $8,500 and sales went from 30 per month to 40? Would you say that demand is elastic, or inelastic? Would total revenue increase or decrease?

$$E = \left|\frac{\%\Delta D}{\%\Delta P}\right|$$

$$\%\Delta P = \frac{(8,500 - 10,000)}{10,000} = -15\%$$

$$\%\Delta D = \frac{(40 - 30)}{30} = .3333 \; or \; 33.3\%$$

$$E = \left|\frac{33.3}{-15}\right| = 2.22$$
so demand is elastic

Since demand is elastic and they lowered price, total revenue should increase.

P1 x Q1 = $10,000 x 30 = $300,000

P2 x Q2 = $8,500 x 40 = $340,000

Example 2:

Simply Cinema reduced the price of their tickets for Tuesday shows from $11 to $7.50. Sales increased from 400 tickets to 500. Is demand elastic, or inelastic? Did their total revenue increase, or decrease?

$$E = \left|\frac{\%\Delta D}{\%\Delta P}\right|$$

$$\%\Delta P = \frac{(7.5 - 11)}{11} = -31.8\%$$

$$\%\Delta D = \frac{(500 - 400)}{400} = 25\%$$

$$E = \left|\frac{25}{-31.8}\right| = .786$$
so demand is inelastic

Since demand is inelastic and they reduced price, total revenue should decrease.

P1 x Q1 = $400 x 11 = $4,400

P2 x Q2 = $500 x 7.5 = $3,750

This illustrated how important it is to have a good idea of the price elasticity of demand for your offering before changing prices.

Markups, Markdowns, and Margins

Markups, markdowns, and margins are all about the difference between what things cost and how much you sell them for. Markups and markdowns are possibly the easiest mathematical task in marketing. However, students often struggle with these because there are different perspectives on them. Margins can also trip you up, unless you are very precise in how the term is being used.

A **margin** is simply the difference between two amounts of money. When marketers talk about margin, they are usually referring to the difference between what a product costs and the price at which it is sold. This is also sometimes referred to as contribution, because that is the amount of money that each unit sold contributes to fixed costs. If you sell enough of them, they begin to contribute to profit. You can also think of it as the difference between the variable costs per unit and the selling price per unit. In the breakeven graph, the margin is what makes total revenue have a steeper slope than total costs. The higher the margin, the steeper the total revenue slope, and the fewer units needed to breakeven.

For instance, if a company buys cell phones for $75 and sells them for $150, their margin is $75. If they only sold them for $125, there margin would be $50, and they would have to sell more to breakeven. The higher the contribution margin, the lower the required quantity to break even.

Impact of Margin on Breakeven Quantity

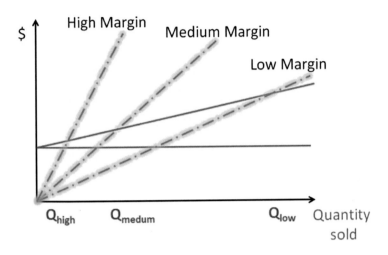

Markup is really just another term for the difference between cost and selling price, or the margin. If you buy cell phones for $75, mark them up $50, and sell them for $125, you have a $50 markup.

P = VC + MU
P – Selling price
VC – Variable costs
MU - Markup

This is all fairly simple, until you start using percentages. The problem is that margin and markup can be applied to either cost or selling price. For example, I knew a young man who went to work at a new job. A new product came in and he asked the store owner how he wanted them priced. He was told they needed a 30% margin. Cost was $50, so he multiplied that times 30%, and used a $15 markup.

Cost $50
Markup   30% (.3 x $50 = $15)
Selling price $65

The next day, the owner accosted him for pricing the products wrong. Confused, the employee responded that he used a 30% margin, as instructed. The owner argued that he had not. The odd thing is, they were both right. The owner showed him the math.

Markup = $15
Selling price = $65
Markup as a percentage of selling price = 15/65 = .231, or **23.1%** -----
NOT 30%

The employ showed him his math.

Markup = $15
Cost = $50
Markup as a percentage of cost = 15/50 = .30, or **30%**

The discrepancy between these two was caused by the different basis they used for markup. One used a percentage markup on selling price, the other on cost. Neither was necessarily wrong. You just have to be sure which markup you want.

MU_P – % Markup on Selling Price = MU/P
MU_C – % Markup on Cost = MU/C

$MU = P(MU_P)$
$MU = C(MU_C)$

If the cost of an item is $75 and you sell it for $100:
Remember, P = C + MU
MU = 100 – 75 = $25
MU_P = MU/P = 25/100 = 25%
MU_C = MU/C = 25/75 = 33.3%

A 33.3% markup on cost, will always give you a 25% markup on selling price, and vice versa.

Examples:

Example 1:
Cost = $200
P = $350
What is the markup as a percentage of selling price (MU_p)?
MU = P − C = 350 − 200 = 150
MU_p = MU/P = 150/350 = .4285 or 42.9%

What is the markup as a percentage of cost (MU_c)?
MU = P − C = 350 − 200 = 150
MU_c = MU/C = 150/200 = .75 or 75%

Example 2:
C = $50
If you want a 25% markup on cost, what would your selling price be?
MU_c = MU/C
25% = MU/50
MU = 12.50
P = C + MU = 50 + 12.50 = $62.50
What would the resulting markup on Price be?
MU_p = MU/P = 12.50/62.50 = .20 or 20%

Example 3:
C = $75
If you want a 25% markup on selling price, what would your selling price be?
MU_p = MU/P − so MU = P(MU_p) = .25P
P = C + MU = 75 + .25P
P − .25P = 75
.75P = 75 − so P = $100
(100 − 75)/100 = 25%, so that must be right.
What would the resulting markup on Cost be?
MU_c = MU/C = 25/75 = .333 or 33.3%

Example 4:

C = $300

If you want a 25% markup on cost, what would your selling price be?

$MU_c = MU/C$ – so MU = $C(MU_c)$ = .25($300) = $75

P = C + MU = 300 + 75

P = $375

What would the resulting markup on Selling Price be?

$MU_P = MU/P$ = (375 – 300)/375 = .20 or 20%

Contribution Margin

The contribution margin is usually expressed as a percentage, although it can be expressed as an actual amount. For instance, if cost is $70 and selling price is $100, the contribution margin is 30%, or $30. Contribution margin, expressed as a percentage, is always the same as markup on selling price. Your contribution margin, as a percentage, will always be lower than your markup on cost, since they use different denominators. In the example above, markup on cost is 30/70, or 42.9%, as compared to 30/100, or 30%, contribution margin.

In terms of breakeven, the contribution margin determines how many units must be sold to reach the breakeven point. The higher the contribution margin, the steeper the total revenue slope, and the fewer units needed to break even. However, it's important to remember that as price goes up, demand goes down, so you can't simply increase the contribution margin to generate the number you'd like to have.

Markdowns

Once you have established a selling price, or list price, you may want to offer discounts, or markdowns, on that price. Markdowns are much simpler than markups, but still require some thought. Markdowns are usually stated as a percentage of selling price, or a specific amount.

DP – Discounted Price

P – Price before Markdown

$MD_\$$ – Amount of price reduction (e.g., $10)

$DP = P - MD_\$$

If the markdown is stated as a percentage of price (e.g., 30%), we can use:

MD_P – Markdown as a percentage of price

$MD_P = MD_\$ / P$ so $MD_\$ = P(MD_P)$

$DP = P - MD_\$ = P - P(MD_P) = P(1 - MD_P)$
This means that a 30% markdown results in a discounted price that is 70% of list price

Examples:

If selling price is $100 and we want to mark it down 30% -

$DP = P(1 - MD_P) = 100(1 - 30\%) = \$70$ so the discounted price is $70

Another way to look at this is:

$MD_P = P(MD_P) = 100(30\%) = \$30$ so the discount is $30

$100 - $30 = $70

One important thing to remember when taking markdowns is the impact on demand and total revenue. You should have a specific objective for your markdowns and be sure that your new price will achieve those objectives. There are many valid reasons for taking markdowns. You may want to clear out inventory at the end of the season, increase store traffic, promote sales of complementary products, or simply increase overall revenue and profits. It's important to remember that the effectiveness of markdowns depends upon the price elasticity of demand. If demand is inelastic, markdowns will decrease total revenue. If demand is elastic, markdowns will increase total revenue.

Multiple markdowns: What does 50/10/5 Mean?

Trade discounts are markdowns given within the channel of distribution. For instance, the discount a manufacturer gives a distributor, or the discount a distributor gives the retailer. It is very common for manufacturers, or resellers, to quote a list price and discount that significantly to members of the channel of distribution. The assumption is that the list price is the suggested retail and the discount represents the profit to be made in the channel. The purchaser does not necessarily sell at the list price, but it serves as a reference point.

The amount of trade discount typically varies from buyer to buyer, depending on the quantities purchased, or services performed. These discounts are often stated sequentially, such as 50/30/10, which means that you get a 50% discount, then a 30% discount, then a 10% discount off of the posted list price. For instance, a manufacturer might have a particular item of furniture with a list price of $1,000 and discount that 50/30/10 to a national retail chain, 50/30 to a smaller, local chain, and 50% to individual retail stores. Sometimes your discount with a supplier is based on the previous quarter's purchases, with minimum thresholds for different levels of discounts. I have often seen companies make large purchases close to the end of a quarter, just to ensure their discount on future purchases.

It's important to recognize what that 50/30/10 discount really means. It doesn't mean you get 90% off of list price (50+30+10), because each discount is applied sequentially. We can illustrate with that $1,000 piece of furniture.

First, you get **50%**:
$1,000 x 50% = $500
$1,000 − $500 = $500

Then, you get **30%**:
$500 x 30% = $150
$500 - $150 = $350

> Then, you get **10%**:
> $350 x 10% = $35
> $350 - $35 = $315

> – Which is what you would pay with a 50/30/10 discount

Your total markdown would be $1,000 - $315 = $685 or 68.5%

If you sold the piece for list price ($1,000), your contribution margin would be $685, or 68.5%.

A retailer who received a 50/30 discount, would pay $350, or a 65% markdown.

A retailer who received 50% would pay $500, a 50% markdown.

Another easy way to calculate your price is to multiply together the percentage you would pay at each step, one minus the discount.

$(1 - .5) \times (1 - .3) \times (1 - .1) = .315$, so you would pay 31.5% of list price

Example:

If you are selling table lamps with a $150 list price, what is your contribution margin, if your discount is 40/20/10?

$150 x **40%** = $60
$150 - $60 = $90

> $90 x **20%** = $18
> $90 - $18 = $72

> > $72 x **10%** = $7.20
> > $72 - $7.20 = $64.80 so you would pay $64.80

If you sell at list price, your contribution on each is:

$150 - $64.80 = $85.20

Your contribution margin, as a percentage is:

$85.20/$150 = .568 or 56.8%

To check that:

(1 - .4) x (1 - .2) x (1 - .1) = .432, so you would pay 43.2% of list price.

That means that your contribution margin would be (1 – 43.2%), or 56.8%

Trade Credit Markdowns

It is very common for businesses selling to businesses (B to B, B2B) to extend short-term credit to their customers, called trade credit. Buyers have a set time to pay, typically 30, 60, or 90 days. This gives them time to resell the goods, or produce something with them and sell the product, generating cash-flow to pay for them. When trade credit is extended, it is also very common to offer a discount for paying before the invoice is due. For instance, 2/10 net 30 means that the invoice must be paid within 30 days, but if it is paid in ten days, or less, a 2% discount may be taken.

For instance, on a $500 invoice, with terms 2/10 net 30, you can pay $490 within ten days, or $500 on the 11th through 30th day.

$500 – ($500 x 2%) = $490

3/10 net 45, for example, would mean you can take a 3% discount if paid within 10 days, but you have 45 days to pay the full amount. On a $500 purchase, this would mean:

$500 – ($500 x 3%) = $485 within ten days

Trade credit and early payment discounts can help both buyers and sellers. Trade credit helps businesses buying the products manage their cash flow. A company that buys $500,000 each year, on 30-day terms, is extended about $41,000 in credit.

500,000/365 x 30 = $41,096

Offering the early payment discounts helps the cash flow of the selling firm. Receiving payments in 10 days, as opposed to 30 days, means they have more cash on hand.

This practice is very common. When I was operating small businesses, most of my vendors offered 2/10 net 30, or similar terms. When I ask small businesses whether they take the discount, or the extra time to pay, most of them tell me they wait 30 days, because it's only 2%. So, the question is, as a purchaser, should you take the early discount? The answer is in the math!

Let's assume you are a small to medium business, buying $500,000 each year on 2/10 net 30 terms.

Your average purchases per day is 500/365 = $1,370

You can pay on the 10th and still get the discount. If you don't take the discount, you are paying for 20 days of credit.

Amount borrowed = (20 days) x $1,370 = $27,397

If your purchases and payments were perfectly uniform, divided across the days of the year, your accounts payable would always be $27,397.

Your annual cost is 2% of $500,000, or $10,000.

That means your true cost of not taking the 2% discount is

$10,000/$27,397 = .365, or 36.5% ----- *that is expensive money*

Unless you are in a cash flow crisis, take those early payment discounts. Pay on the 10th day, or whichever the deadline is, and get the discount. If you don't pay on the 10th day, though, don't pay until the deadline, because you have already paid to use the money for the full term.

As a seller, offering the discount is a great deal for you. If you have a customer who purchases $100,000 in product from you, taking the full 30 days to pay, you would be lending them about $8,219, for which you would receive 2% extra, or $2,000.

Allowing this customer to take 30 days to pay would mean that you invest $8,219 in extended credit. If they always take 30 days to pay, they would pay $2,000 per year for that privilege.

$100,000/365 x 30 = $8,219.18

$100,000 x 2% = $2,000

So, you would earn about $2,000/$8,219 = .243 or 24.3% on your investment

In reality, you are only lending the money for an extra 20 days, so the result is even better.

$100,000/365 x 20 = $5,749.45

$100,000 x 2% = $2,000

So, you would earn about $2,000/$5,749 = .348 or 34.8% on your investment

Trade credit is a tool that offers benefits on both sides of the transaction. From a purchasing standpoint, the extended term (30, 60, or 90 days) can be helpful in managing temporary cash-flow problems. But, it should never be your long-term payment strategy.

Customer Lifetime Value (CLV)

Customer lifetime value (CLV) is a concept that recognizes both current and future purchases. It is the net value of all the purchases a customer will make from your brand, now and in the future. It recognizes that the true value of a customer is much more than what they will spend on any single transaction. Properly calculated, it can tell you the net present value of all the future business you will do with an average customer. The actual calculations can become fairly complex, but there are formulae in Microsoft Excel and many online applications that simplify them for you. What is really important is understanding the concept of CLV, rather than mastering the calculations.

It is useful in many ways, one of which is setting a limit on how much you should be willing to spend to acquire a new customer. You certainly don't want to spend more than the value they will add, but you also don't want to miss out on new customers, because you aren't willing to spend enough. It can also be used to evaluate the relative worth of different types of customers you may have. For instance, if you are an automobile brand, how much more is a customer worth who buys a new car every two years, as compared to a customer who keeps her car for six years? This can tell you how much you should be willing to spend to change that purchase behavior.

The formulae used to calculate CLV vary from very simple, to very complex. Since they are all based on predicting future behaviors, you have to decide what level of complexity meets your needs. The basis of CLV is your net profit on each sale. If a customer spends $1,000 each year with you and your costs of goods sold are $750, then their value in that year is $250. But hopefully, they'll keep buying from you in future years.

The simplest CLV calculations ignore the time value of money and customer attrition, simply multiplying the average annual profit times the number of years they will remain a customer. For the example above, assume the following:

Average spending per year: $1,000
Time as customers: 20 years
Costs of goods sold: $750
CLV = (1,000 – 750) x 20 = $5,000

That's a good starting point, but one problem is that not all customers will stick around for 20 years. The first improvement should be to adjust for customer retention. While we can't know which specific customers will leave, we know the percentage of customers who leave each year. We can apply that to all the customers, to adjust their average lifetime value. Let's assume that we lose 20% of customers each year, retaining 80%.

The first year, the average customer is worth $250, but the second year 20% of those are gone. So, the average customer is only worth $200 the second year ($250 x 80%) and only worth $160 the third year ($250 x 80% x 80%). Taking customer attrition into account, CLV is the sum of the average customer value for the next 20 years. The table below shows the average customer value, for the next twenty years, adjusted for 80% retention.

If you add up the average value each year for 20 years, the average customer is worth about $1,236. Notice that 19 years from now the average customer of today is only worth $3.60, due to attrition. This is even smaller when we discount for time. This is why you seldom see net present value calculations carried out beyond 20 years. In equation form:

$$CLV = \sum_{k=1}^{20} 250(.8)^{k-1}$$

Years from Now	Value	Years from Now	Value
0	$ 250.00	10	$ 26.84
1	$ 200.00	11	$ 21.47
2	$ 160.00	12	$ 17.18
3	$ 128.00	13	$ 13.74
4	$ 102.40	14	$ 11.00
5	$ 81.92	15	$ 8.80
6	$ 65.54	16	$ 7.04
7	$ 52.43	17	$ 5.63
8	$ 41.94	18	$ 4.50
9	$ 33.55	19	$ 3.60

This is more realistic, and provides a better spending guideline. If you spent $1,500 to acquire the average customer, but only retained 80% of them each year, you would slowly go out of business. Even this formula still ignores the fact that money received in the future is worth less now than money received now. To be more accurate we need to discount the profit per customer from future years. We need the net present value of all those future cash flows, discounted for the time that has passed. Remember that $250 received one year from now is only worth about $240 today, assuming a fair interest rate of 4%. The formula for discounting cash flows is:

$$Present\ value = \frac{X}{(1+r)^t}$$

Where: X = cash flow

r = discount rate

t = number of periods until the cash flow

So, the equation becomes:

$$CLV = \sum_{k=1}^{20} \frac{250(.8)^{k-1}}{(1+r)^{k-1}}$$

If we use a discount rate of 4%, the average customer lifetime value drops from $1,236 to about $1,078.

Overall spending was $250 x 20 years, or $5,000. When we account for 20% annual customer attrition, that drops to $1,236. When we account for the time value of money, the average customer lifetime value is $1,078. This gives us a reference point for spending on customer acquisition, or evaluating strategies designed to improve retention or increase spending.

Whichever formula you use, at whatever level of precision you attempt, CLV calculations always involve some assumptions, and will never be precisely correct. The most important aspect is that you understand the concept and recognize two important facts. First, long-term customer relationships increase CLV and are more profitable than transactional relationships. Second, whatever the true CLV is sets a realistic limit on how much you should spend to acquire and retain customers.

Diagnostics

There are numerous different metrics available to evaluate your firm's performance and particularly the outcomes of your marketing efforts. Most of these are relatively simple, mathematically, but are powerful tools, when used appropriately.

Market Share

One of the simplest metrics is your share of the market. This is a simple ratio of your sales to total sales in the market, but there are at least two versions. You can calculate market share based on unit sales, or dollar sales. The simple formula is:

$$\frac{Your\ sales}{Total\ Market\ sales}$$

If your offering is priced significantly differently than the market average, your unit share can be very different from your dollar share. In the example below, your firm's offering is priced at $15 each, compared to $10 each for the overall market. As a result, your unit share is only 10%, while your dollar share is 15%, 50% higher. Neither of these is the "right" market share to use. It is important that you consider both of these calculated shares when evaluating performance.

	Units	Dollars
Your sales	10,000	$150,000
Market Sales	100,000	$1,000,000
Your share	10%	15%

Also, as with many metrics, the trend in your market share may tell you much more about your performance than your share at any one point in time.

Example:

Consider a company selling mobile phones. The Tsunami 7 sells for $295 and they sold 20,000 of them last month. If a total of 110,000 mobile phones were sold and total dollar sales were $15,950,000, what was their market share?

Their share in units is:

$$\frac{20,000}{110,000} = 18.2\%$$

Their share in dollars is:

$$\frac{(295 \times 20,000)}{15,950,000} = 37\%$$

The reason for the difference, is that their phone sells for just over twice the price of an average phone.

$$\text{Average phone price} = \frac{15,950,000}{110,000} = \$145$$

It's important not only to be able to calculate your market share, but to interpret it's meaning. In this case, it would depend on the company's current goals and objectives. If their goal is to penetrate the market, they might consider discounting their phones. If their objective is to optimize current profits, their current pricing may be a great strategy.

Awareness

One of the most critical measures of brand health is awareness among your target market. As with other marketing measures, the calculations are fairly simple, but you need to be precise in the application.

Awareness is typically measured as the percentage of people who are aware of your brand divided by the total number of people in the market.

$$Awareness = \frac{\# \ Aware}{\# \ in \ the \ Market}$$

We typically measure this by surveying a representative sample of the population and generalizing those results to the general population of our target market. One twist is that you really need to know two different types of awareness, unaided and aided. Unaided awareness is just what it says, those consumers can name your brand with no help. For instance, we might ask people to name all the brands of detergent they can think of. If we surveyed 200 people and 182 of them listed Tide, then Tide's unaided awareness among that population would be:

$$Unaided \ Awareness = \frac{174}{200} = 87\%$$

You can use this number to compare different brands to your brand's awareness, or compare your awareness among different market segments. For instance, in the example above, if 50 of the respondents were under 34 and only 30 of them listed Tide, Tide's awareness among those under 34 would only be:

$$Unaided \ Awareness, under \ 34 = \frac{30}{50} = 60\%$$

For those people who list your brand when prompted by the category (soap, canned soup, autos, etc.) we say that the brand is in their evoked set. The brand is evoked when the category is given. Sometimes, people who can't list your brand without help may still be aware of it, if reminded. When we ask about awareness while providing a prompt, we call this aided awareness. We might ask those people who did not list Tide how familiar they are with a list of brands including Tide. If an additional 22 people responded that they have heard of Tide, then the aided awareness would be:

$$Aided \ Awareness = \frac{(174 + 22)}{200} = 98\%$$

For consumers who recognize the brand, but could not list it on their own, we say the brand is in their awareness set. They are aware of it, but it does not come to mind when thinking about the product category. Though simple, these measures are critical to brand success. Your brand must make it into the awareness set, then the evoked set, before it can be in the consideration set and have a chance of being chosen.

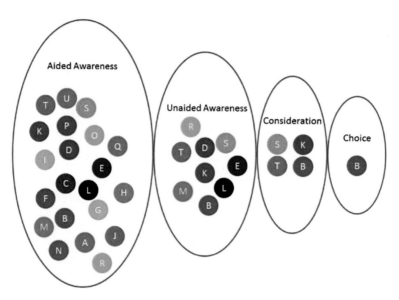

Conversion Rate

Another important metric is your conversion rate. Unlike your market share, which is an overall measure of success, conversion rates typically refer to a specific marketing effort, or opportunity. Conversion rates can be calculated in a number of different instances. The key concept is that you convert people from one stage to another: shoppers to buyers; viewers to clickers; lurkers to posters. In online environments you may want to calculate your conversion rate for people who view an ad for your site.

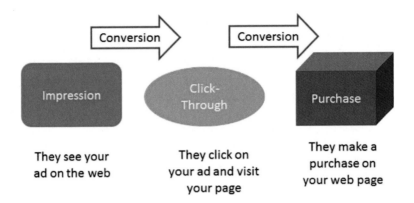

The actual math is very simple.

$$\text{Conversion Rate} = \frac{\# \ Converted}{Total \ \#}$$

As an example, we can apply some actual data to the diagram above:

In response to an ad campaign, we had the following results:
Unique Impressions = 4,287 (This is the number of visitors who saw the ad.)
Click-Through = 176 (This is the number who clicked on the ad.)

$$\text{Conversion Rate} = \frac{176}{4,287} = .041 = 4.1\%$$

Another example might be converting shoppers to buyers in a brick-and-mortar retail store.

Shopper entering the store = 362
Shoppers making a purchase = 123

$$\text{Conversion Rate} = \frac{123}{362} = 34\%$$

The question is, are those good conversion rates? That can be a difficult question to answer. You can typically find statistics for conversion rates using online search engines. Those will give you a benchmark for comparison. However, a direct comparison may not be fair. If your brand is new to the market, you might expect lower conversion rates. The best answer may be to track those conversion rates over time and establish a trend. You may also use conversion rates to compare different versions of an ad, or different levels of discounting. For instance, if you ran two online ads, you could compare conversion rates to evaluate their relative effectiveness.

Marketing Return on Investment (MROI)

The concept behind your Marketing Return on Investment (MROI) is that your marketing spending should be viewed as an investment and you want a positive return on your investments. There are really two aspects to MROI. The first is short-term effects, such as increased sales. The second is less tangible and longer-term, including brand awareness, positive affect, and other dimensions of brand equity. While the investment in marketing is easy to calculate, the return can be problematic.

While there are many different ways to calculate MROI, the basic formula is:

$$\frac{Additional\ Profit - Marketing\ Costs}{Marketing\ Costs}$$

For example, if a short advertising campaign, costing $10,000, generates $60,000 in additional sales. If we assume a contribution margin of 25%, then:

$60,000 x 25% = $15,000 in marginal profit

$$\frac{\$15,000 - \$10,000}{\$10,000} = .50\ or\ 50\%$$

This means that for every marketing dollar spent, it was recovered, plus an additional 50 cents in profits.

While this seems very straightforward, it can often be difficult to identify which sales should be attributed to the marketing campaign and which would have occurred anyway. This is even more challenging when you are taking the long-term perspective. An ad campaign might generate almost no immediate sales increase, but have a long-term impact on future customer behavior. One tool that might prove helpful in calculating long-term MROI is the Customer Lifetime Value model. In addition to marginal revenue, marketing may reduce the customer turnover rate, which can have a significant impact on profits.

For instance, in the example above, what if sales had only increased by $30,000?

$30,000 x 25% = $7,500 in marginal profit

$$\frac{\$7{,}500 \; - \; \$10{,}000}{\$10{,}000} = -\,.25 \; or - 25\%$$

This means that we only recovered 75 cents for every dollar spent. However, what if it reduced our annual customer attrition from 20% to 15%?

Average spending per year: $200
Time as customers: 10 years
Costs of goods sold: $150
At a retention rate of 80%, CLV = $201

At a retention rate of 85%, CLV = $237, an increase of $36 per customer.

If the firm has 1,000 loyal customers, that is an increase of $36,000 in addition to the increased direct profits. Based on the that, MROI becomes:

$$\frac{\$7{,}500 + \$36{,}000 \; - \; \$10{,}000}{\$10{,}000} = 3.35 \; or \; 335\%$$

That means that every marketing dollar invested would generate $3.35 in additional profits. Once again, the challenge in calculating MROI may be accurately estimating marketing's impact. Even so, MROI can be a valuable tool for evaluating marketing investments, or comparing competing prospective investments.

This is also a good illustration of the synergistic effects of good marketing math. To truly appreciate the impact of marketing investments, you need to consider the overall MROI, which goes beyond short-term sales and includes long-term Customer Lifetime Value.

Summary and Conclusions

Whether we acknowledge it, or not, all marketing strategies depend on mathematical relationships. Elasticity of demand, contribution margins, conversion rates, and other math-based concepts determine the success of marketing. Mastering a few simple calculations can demystify seeming complex relationships and help us avoid pitfalls in the market.

While there are many other calculations that may influence marketing decisions, those covered here provide a good basis. They are also those that I find marketing students struggle with most often. Beyond these basics, you might want to explore, or revisit, basic statistics, t-tests, Chi-squared, regression, etc. Another area of study that is changing how firms market is Big Data, or data analytics, which involves collecting enormous amounts of data on customer behaviors and deriving previously unrecognized relationships.

The basics of marketing are still the same. The brand that gives customers the best experience at a reasonable price will always do well. The challenge is defining what the means for different customers and how to provide it. Marketing math makes that easier.

Thank you for reading this Business Short Book. I hope it met your expectations and you found it enlightening and enjoyable. If so, please take a minute to review it on Amazon.com.

Amazon.com/author/JohnStory

If there was anything you did not like, or think could be improved, please send me your feedback.

JohnStoryResearch@gmail.com

You can find other books similar to this one at:

Amazon.com/author/johnstory

You can see more about me at:

http://StoryedSolutions.com

Glossary

Breakeven – the point at which revenue exactly covers total costs

Contribution – Selling price minus cost to acquire, or produce. This is how much each item sold contributes to covering costs and creating profits.

Contribution Margin – Typically, the contribution as a percentage of selling price.

Conversion rate – the percentage of people who transition from one shopping stage to another, e.g., shoppers to purchasers.

Customer Lifetime Value – The value of all current and future purchases the average customer will make.

Price Elasticity of Demand – a measure of the extent to which changing price results in a change in the quantity demanded.

Margin – the difference between two amounts of money

Markdown – a reduction in the selling price of an item

Marketing Return on Investment (MROI) – the income generated by marketing efforts in excess of the cost of the marketing.

Market Share – the percentage of total market sales made by a firm. The ratio of your firm's sales to total sales within a given time period.

Markup – the difference between the variable cost of a product and the selling price

Trade Credit – extended time allowed to pay an invoice, typically 30, 60, or 90 days. This is often accompanied by an early payment discount. For instance, 2/10 net 60.

Equations Used

Breakeven Analysis

Contribution = P – VC

P – Selling Price

VC – Variable Costs per Unit

$$(P \times Q) = FC + (VC \times Q)$$

Primary Breakeven Equation

Q – Quantity sold

FC – Fixed Costs

Price Elasticity of Demand

$$E = \left| \frac{\%\Delta D}{\%\Delta P} \right|$$

E – Elasticity

$\%\Delta D$ – percentage change in Demand

$\%\Delta P$ – percentage change in Price

Markups and Markdowns

P = VC + MU

P – Selling price

VC – Variable costs

MU – Markup

MU_P – % Markup on Selling Price = MU/P

MU_C – % Markup on Cost = MU/C

DP – Discounted Price

P – Price before Markdown

MD$_\$$ – Amount of price reduction (e.g., \$10)

DP = P – MD$_\$$

MD$_P$ – Markdown as a percentage of price

MDP = MD\$ /P so MD$_\$$ = P(MD$_P$)

DP = P – MD$_\$$ = P – P(MD$_P$) = P(1 - MD$_P$)

Customer Lifetime Value

$$CLV = \sum_{k=1}^{n} Net(R)^{k-1}$$

CLV – Customer Lifetime Value

Net – Annual Spending Less Cost

R – Retention rate

n – Years as a customer

$$CLV = \sum_{k=1}^{n} \frac{Net(R)^{k-1}}{(1+r)^{k-1}}$$

r – Discount rate

Market Share

$$Market\ Share = \frac{Your\ sales}{Total\ Market\ sales}$$

Conversion Rates

$$Conversion\ Rate = \frac{\#\ Converted}{Total\ \#}$$

Marketing Return on Investment

$$MROI = \frac{Additional\ Profit - Marketing\ Costs}{Marketing\ Costs}$$

Examples

Breakeven Analysis

Billy Bob's Brakes sells brakes for cars. Their fixed costs are $30,000 per month. Their variable costs per set of brake shoes is $9. If they sell 10,000 sets of brake shoes per month, how many do they have to sell to break even?

FC = $30,000
VC = $9
Q = 10,000

Let's take two different approaches:

First, how much does each unit need to contribute, in order to cover fixed costs?

30,000/10,000 = $3, so the Markup on each one needs to be $3
P = C + MU
P = 9 + 3 = $12

Now let's use the formula:

(P x Q) = FC + (VC x Q)
10,000P = 30,000 + 10,000(9)
P = 120,000/10,000 = $12

To check our result:
10,000(**12**) = 30,000 + 10,000(9)
120,000 = 120,000

Marjorie's Mattresses has fixed costs of $400,000 per year. Their variable costs per mattress is $120. If they sell them for $220 each, how many must they sell to breakeven?
FC = $400,000
VC = $120

Q = ?

P = 220

(P x Q) = FC + (VC x Q)

220Q = 400,000 + 120Q

220Q – 120Q = 400,000

Q = 400,000/100 = **4,000**

If each mattress contributes \$100, you need to sell 4,000 of them to break even.

(220)4,000 = 400,000 + 120(4,000)

880,000 = 880,000

The Tinhorn Bar and Grill has \$10,000 per month in fixed costs. They mark variable costs up 100%, so VC is 50% of selling price. How much must they sell each month to break even?

This may seem confusing at first. Students often tell me they don't have enough information. The solution is to put everything you have into the formula.

(P x Q) = FC + (VC x Q)

P(Q) = 30,000 + .5P(Q)

(P - .5P)Q = 30,000

.5P(Q) = 30,000

P(Q) = 60,000

So, they must do \$60,000 in revenue each month to break even.

Notice that we don't need to know what they are selling, just what their contribution margin is. This is helpful when calculating breakeven for something like a restaurant that sells a variety of different menu items, at different prices. It works, as long as you know the average contribution margin.

Wendy's Widgets has $2,000,000 in fixed costs. They are on track to sell 500,000 widgets this year. Their variable cost per widget is $4. If they sell them for $9 each, will they break even?

There are several ways to approach this. The first is to calculate the required volume (Q) to break even.
(P x Q) = FC + (VC x Q)
9(Q) = 2,000,000 + 4(Q)
(9 - 4)Q = 2,000,000
Q = 400,000 ------- since they will sell 500,000 they will do even better than break even and have a profit.

The second approach is to calculate the required selling price to break even.
(P x Q) = FC + (VC x Q)
P(500,000) = 2,000,000 + 4(500,000)
P = $8 ------ since they are selling them for $9, they will do even better than bread even and have a profit.

The third approach is to go all the way back to the original profit equation
Profit = (P x Q) – [FC + (VC x Q)]
Profit = 9(500,000) – [2,000,000 + 4(500,000)]
Profit = 4,500,000 – 4,000,000
Profit = 500,000
This makes sense, since they are selling an extra 100,000 units above breakeven and they contribute $5 each.

What if, Wendy's Widgets had a target of $200,000 in profits, at 500,000 units sold?
FC = $2,000,000
Profit - $200,000
VC = $4
Q = 500,000
P = ?

(P x Q) = FC + (VC x Q)
P(500,000) = 2,000,000 + 200,000 + 4(500,000)
P = $8.40 ------ if they sold them for $8.40 they would have a profit of $200,000

Price Elasticity of Demand

If Betty's Burger Joint reduces all of their prices by 20% and sales increase by 30%, is demand elastic, or inelastic?

Just looking at this, you know demand is elastic, because the percentage change in demand (30%) is greater than the percentage change in price (20%).

Let's do the calculation and check:

$$E = \left|\frac{\%\Delta D}{\%\Delta P}\right|$$

$$E = \left|\frac{30}{20}\right| = 1.5$$

Since E > 1, demand is elastic.

What if she had increased the prices 20% and demand fell 15%?

Since the percentage change in demand is less than the percentage change in price, we know that demand is inelastic.

$$E = \left|\frac{\%\Delta D}{\%\Delta P}\right|$$

$$E = \left|\frac{-15}{20}\right| = .75$$

Since E < 1, demand is inelastic.

Mike's Motors ran a sale last month. They reduced the average selling price on their cars and trucks from $22,000 to $18,500. Their average monthly sales are 15 cars, but last month they sold 20 cars. Would you say demand is elastic, or inelastic?

$$E = \left| \frac{\%\Delta D}{\%\Delta P} \right|$$

$$\%\Delta P = \frac{(18{,}500 - 22{,}000)}{22{,}000} = -15.9\%$$

$$\%\Delta D = \frac{(20 - 15)}{15} = .3333 \; or \; 33.3\%$$

$$E = \left| \frac{33.3}{-15.9} \right| = 2.1 \quad \text{so demand is elastic}$$

Since demand is elastic and they lowered price, total revenue should increase.

P1 x Q1 = $22,000 x 15 = $330,000

P2 x Q2 = $18,500 x 20 = $370,000

So, they increased revenue by $40,000. Notice that you can't tell what impact this had on profits, since you don't know their variable costs.

Wild, Wet, and Woolly is a family water park where you can bring your pets. They have been dissatisfied with their financial performance, so they increased ticket prices 15%. Ticket sales went from 4,200 per day to 4,000 per day. Do you think their strategy worked?

$$E = \left| \frac{\%\Delta D}{\%\Delta P} \right|$$

$$\%\Delta P = 15\%$$

$$\%\Delta D = \frac{(4{,}000 - 4{,}200)}{4{,}200} = -4.8\%$$

$$E = \left| \frac{-4.8}{15} \right| = \quad .32 \text{ so demand is inelastic}$$

Since demand is inelastic and they increased price, total revenue should increase.

To test this, we can pick a random ticket price, of say $10

P1 x Q1 = $10 x 4,200 = $42,000

P2 x Q2 = $11.5 x 4,000 = $46,000

Revenue increased and costs are similar, or lower, so this probably worked out for them.

Markups and Markdowns

Pauline sells pets. If she wants a 40% markup on cost, at what price should she sell a tortoise, for which she pays $80? And, what contribution margin would that give her, as a percentage?

P = C + MU

P = C + 40%(C)

P = 80 + .4(80) = $112

Her contribution would be 112 – 80 = 32

Her markup on selling price, which is the same as contribution margin, would be:

$$\frac{32}{112} = .286 \; or \; 28.6\%$$

So, a 40% markup on cost results in a 28.6% markup on selling price.

What if Pauline decided that 28.6% was not sufficient, that she needed a 40% contribution margin, or markup on selling price? At what price would she need to sell the tortoise for which she paid $80?

P = C + MU

P = C + 40%(P)

P = 80 + .4P

.6P = 80

P = $133.33

To check this:

MU = P − C = 133.33 − 80 = 53.33

$$MU_P = \frac{MU}{P} = \frac{53.33}{133.33} = 40\%$$

What would the markup on cost be?

$$MU_C = \frac{MU}{C} = \frac{53.33}{80} = 66.67\%$$

So, if you mark cost up 2/3, you get a 40% contribution margin.

_____

If Columbus Hardware gets a 40/10/5 markdown on aluminum windows, how much would they pay for a window, if the list price is $360?

360 − 360(40%) = 216

216 − 216(10%) = 194.40

194.40 − 194.4(5%) = 184.68

So, they would pay 184.68. If they sold it at list price, $360, their contribution margin would be:

$$\frac{360 - 184.68}{360} = 48.7\%$$

Another way to approach this problem:

If their discount is 40/10/5, they would pay $(1 - .4)(1 - .1)(1 - .05) =$ 51.3% of list price.

$.513(360) = 184.68$

On November 10, Pauline's Pets receives an invoice for $480 with terms 2/10 net 30. If she pays it by the 20th, how much should she pay? What if she waits until December 5?

If she pays within 10 days, she should take the 2% discount and pay $480(.98) = 470.40

If she waits until after 10 days, but within the 30-day term, she should pay $480.

Market Share

Frank's Fabulous Flowers sold $22,000 worth of flowers last month. If total sales in his market area were $186,000, what was his market share?

$$\frac{\$22,000}{\$186,000} = 11.8\%$$

Charisma Car Sales sold 320 cars last year, at an average price of $18,400 each. If total sales in their market were 3,850 cars, for a total of $66,220,00, what was their market share in dollars and units?

Unit share $= \dfrac{320}{3,850} = 8.3\%$

Their total dollar sales were 320 x 18,400 = $5,888,000

So, their dollar share was:

$$\frac{5,888,000}{66,220,000} = 8.9\%$$

We can see if that makes sense by comparing their average selling price with the market average:

$$\frac{66,220,000}{3,850} = 17,200$$

Since their average unit price, $18,400 is higher than the market average, $17,200, it makes sense that their share of total dollar sales would be higher than their share of units sold.

Betty and Johnny have an ice cream shop in a small town, where there are two other ice cream shops. Their sales last month were $28,000. They know from previous research that their prices are about 20% less than the market average. According to the Chamber of Commerce, total ice cream shop sales last month were $72,000. What is their market share in dollars and units?

The dollar share is easy:

$$\frac{\$28,000}{\$72,000} = 38.9\%$$

To find their unit share, we can simply pick an average selling price. If their average price is $4, then we can find the market average selling price:

B&J's price = .8(Market Average) so Market Average = B&J's price/.8

Assume a price of $4 for B&J, the Market Average is $5

That would mean that total market sales were $72,000/5 = 14,400

B&J's unit sales were $28,000/4 = 7,000

Their unit market share is then 7,000/14,400 = 48.6%

(It doesn't matter what price you choose, as long as B&Js price is 80% of the market average)

Conversion Rates

Frank's Fantastic Flowers is examining the results of a recent ad campaign. They had 8,274 impressions, 172 of those people clicked on the ad and visited their website, and 11 people placed an order.

What is their conversion rate from Impressions to Click-throughs?

$$\frac{172}{8,274} = .021 \; or \; 2.1\%$$

What is their conversion rate from Page Views to Purchase?

$$\frac{11}{172} = .064 \; or \; 6.4\%$$

What is their conversion rate from Impressions to Purchases?

$$\frac{11}{8,274} = .00133 \; or \; .133\%$$

You can get this same result by multiplying the conversion rates for impressions to click-through and click-through to purchase.

$$(.021).064) = .00134$$

You can use this result to estimate how many impressions they need to generate a purchase.

$$\frac{1}{.00133} = 751.9$$

So, they need to generate about 750 impressions for each purchase.

ABOUT THE AUTHOR

I was born in 1957 in Houston, Texas. I had a long career in the oilfields of South Texas, before going back to earn a business degree from Texas A&M University. Though I started as Class of '80, I finished as Class of '91. One of my favorite T-shirts says, "College, the 12 best years of my life!" and I mean it. Once I started back, I found it difficult to stop, earning an MS from A&M and a Ph. D. from the University of Colorado. I have served on the faculty of UTSA, Idaho State University, and the University of St. Thomas, in Houston. I have worked with a variety of marketing research firms to measure, analyze, and develop customer/brand relationships. I founded Storyed Solutions to provide marketing and management research solutions to industry and higher education. I have been married for over 30 years, to the same wife, and have three lovely daughters.

My Business Short Books compile material that I have used to supplement my teaching and give students a deeper understanding of specific strategic topics. They include insights, examples, and equations (when appropriate). They are not designed to replace textbooks, but convey a level of understanding not typically available from the typical textbook chapter.

I learned to surf, at 49, when we decided to move back to Texas, from Idaho. It was one of the best decisions I ever made. In Old Guy Surfing I share my learning experiences, along with strategies and techniques to keep old guys surfing into old age.

See more at:

Amazon.com/author/johnstory

or

http://StoryedSolutions.com

40771873R00034

Made in the USA
Middletown, DE
22 February 2017